PupStyle

Sticker Book

By Dara Foster

SCHOLASTIC INC.

This city slicker pooch is just the right size for sprinting through crowded urban sidewalks and squeezing into hip doggy cafés. But some pups prefer the wide-open spaces of the countryside to run and roam. It's true: City life just isn't for everyone.

LONG-HAIRED CHIHUAHUA

MINIATURE SCHNAUZER

What pooch doesn't enjoy picnicking in the park? During the dog days of summer, pups may love to run around and refuel, but certain common foods, such as chocolate, avocados, and grapes, are dangerous for dogs. It's best to stick to the puppy chow.

ENGLISH BULLDOG

Humans aren't the only ones who like to doggy-paddle. Some canines make excellent swimmers, especially breeds with webbed feet. Three dogs—two Pomeranians and a Pekingese—even survived the sinking of the *Titanic*!

Even short-legged shih tzus know how to shake it on the dance floor. Across the globe, pups compete in dance competitions called "canine freestyles." In some countries, like Italy, there are doggy discos for people who want to bust a move with their mutt!

SHIH TZU

This pooch might look calm and relaxed, but don't let her fool you. Although pet dogs are mainly gentle, they have some pretty wild ancestors: wolves!

LONG-HAIRED POMERANIAN

YORKIE

Most canines, like this hip Yorkie, are known for their cool and easygoing personalities. But that doesn't mean they never break a sweat. Although dogs don't perspire the same way humans do, all pooches sweat in at least one place—between their paw pads!

KLEE KAI

Even hot dogs need cold-weather gear. When temperatures drop, dogs rely on their coats to keep them warm and stylin'. Other important winter wear? Jewelry. Since pups can easily get lost in the snow, dog tags are a must.

Step aside, Sherlock Holmes. These crime-busting canines can track scents in the air and on the ground. A dog's sense of smell is about 1,000 times stronger than a person's! No wonder pooches make such terrific police partners.

SCHNAUZER-MALTESE MIX

Check out this healthy hound. Whether it involves taking a long walk, playing fetch, or going for a swim, exercise is important for dogs of all sizes. Even small dogs can pack some major muscle. The Jack Russell terrier has been known to stand up to dogs ten times its tiny size!

MI-KI

LONG-HAIRED CHIHUAHUA

Who says you can't teach an old dog new tricks? The average pup is about as smart as a two-year-old child. This means a full-grown dog can understand around 165 human words! That's a lot of tricks.

Singing in the rain isn't for everyone—and neither is barking. Many dogs don't like raindrops because the sound hurts their sensitive ears. Dogs can hear about ten times better than humans!

Houston, we have a pooch. Dogs were flown into Earth's orbit before any other living creature—even humans! Because dogs make such great explorers, they're often trained to search for and rescue other animals and people in danger.

DACHSHUND MIX

Happy birthday, pup! Dogs age much faster than humans. The first two years in a dog's life are like twenty-four human years! Small and midsize canines, like this Boston terrier, generally have the longest life spans. More birthdays mean more cake!

BOSTON TERRIER

POMERANIAN

Dogs can get some of the same diseases people get—and they can smell those diseases, too! In fact, pups can help humans stay healthy. People who own pets have less stress and tend to live longer. Pups really do make the perfect caretaker when you're sick as a, well, dog.

LONG-HAIRED CHIHUAHUA

Yee-haw! Some dogs are bred to work on farms. But when this canine cowgirl isn't busy working, she's probably off sneaking treats somewhere else. Most full-grown dogs don't like milk, as many are allergic to dairy.